YOUR NUMBER'S UP

Digits, number lines, negative and positive numbers

Rob Colson

W
FRANKLIN WATTS
LONDON • SYDNEY

Acknowledgments and Picture credits

First published Great Britain in 2016 by
The Watts Publishing Group

Copyright © The Watts Publishing Group,
2016

All rights reserved.

Series editor: Sarah Peutrill

Produced by Tall Tree Ltd
Design: Ben Ruocco
Consultants: Hilary Koll and Steve Mills

Every attempt has been made to
clear copyright. Should there be any
inadvertent omission please apply to the
publisher for rectification.

Dewey Classification 513.1'5

ISBN: 978 1 4451 4941 7
Printed in China

Franklin Watts
An imprint of
Hachette Children's Group
Part of The Watts Publishing Group
Carmelite House
50 Victoria Embankment
London EC4Y 0DZ

An Hachette UK Company
www.hachette.co.uk

www.franklinwatts.co.uk

Picture credits:
t-top, b-bottom, l-left, r-right, c-centre,
front cover-fc, back cover-bc
All images courtesy of Dreamstime.com,
unless indicated:
Inside front Maciej Dvorak; fctr, 1, 4b,
14l, Leisuretime70; 4b, 22b
Andreadonetti; fcc, 5t, 16c, 23bl
Vectorlibellule; 5b Reshoot; 6b
Lespalenik; bcc, 7c Doomko; 9t Gekaskr;
9t iStockphoto.com/Linda Steward;
9b Muuraa/Lhfgraphics; fcbr, 11t
Tuulijumala; 12c, 25b Mexrix; 15t
Manaemedia; fctr, 17c, 23, 29t Mzwonko;
17b Elnur; 18cl Radub85; 18b NASA;
19t NASA; 19c, 31t Linqong; 20b, 32t
Stylephotographs; 23tr Macrovector; bctr,
24t Eraxion; bctl, 24b Inna Esina; fctc,
25b Indigofish; 27b, 30t Macrovector;
30c Fixzma

Contents

How do we count?

Early humans used the fingers on one hand to count up to five. We still count in bunches of five when we keep tallies. To make a tally on one hand, count up to four using your fingers, then cross off five with the thumb.

Using both our hands, we can count up to 10. This is why we count with 10 digits.

Counting the days

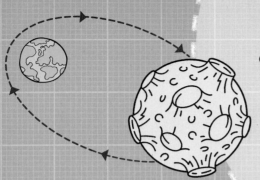

The earliest record of a human counting over 10 comes from Africa. A baboon bone was found in the Lebombo Mountains in Swaziland with 29 marks on it. Scientists think that it may have been used as a calendar, keeping track of the Moon's phases (a lunar month is 29 days long). The bone is more than 35,000 years old.

Machine for counting

An abacus looks simple, but experts can use it to perform complicated sums quickly. Each column of beads represents a power of 10. A bead pulled down from the top represents five, while each bead pulled up from the bottom represents one.

The number on the abacus above is

5 9 9 0 2 6

Numbers
that come
naturally

The numbers we use for counting things are called the counting numbers (also known as the natural numbers).

1 2 3 4 5 6 7 8 9 10

Even or odd

Counting numbers are all either even or odd. Even numbers are multiples of 2.

Even numbers of things can be divided into two equal groups.

Many streets have houses with odd numbers on one side of the road and even numbers on the other side.

51   53   55

52   54

Prime numbers

Prime numbers are special numbers that can only be divided by 1 and themselves. Ancient Greek mathematician Eratosthenes came up with a trick for finding all the primes between 1 and 100. It is called the Sieve of Eratosthenes.

- Numbers divisible by 2 are coloured red.
- Numbers divisible by 3 are coloured green.
- Numbers divisible by 5 are coloured purple.
- Numbers divisible by 7 are coloured orange.
- Every other number (in white) is a prime.

1	2	3	4	5	6	7	8	9	10
11	12	13	14	15	16	17	18	19	20
21	22	23	24	25	26	27	28	29	30
31	32	33	34	35	36	37	38	39	40
41	42	43	44	45	46	47	48	49	50
51	52	53	54	55	56	57	58	59	60
61	62	63	64	65	66	67	68	69	70
71	72	73	74	75	76	77	78	79	80
81	82	83	84	85	86	87	88	89	90
91	92	93	94	95	96	97	98	99	100

Six frogs can divide into two groups of three.

Odd numbers of things can be lined up with one in the middle.

57

59

A history of nothing

Can you solve the following equation:

You probably know that the answer is 0 (zero). Zero is familiar to us today, but for thousands of years, mathematicians had to do all their calculations without a number for nothing.

Holding a place

We need zero to write down large numbers. Zero is used as a 'placeholder', showing that there is no quantity of that size. For example, look at the number 406:

Hundreds **4**   Tens **0**   Units **6**

Take away the zero and you have the much smaller number 46.

Tens **4**   Units **6**

The zero holds the other digits in their correct places.

406

Brahmagupta's Rules

no. 1

$$A + 0 = A$$

no. 2

$$A - 0 = A$$

no. 3

$$A \times 0 = 0$$

no. 4

$$A \div 0 = 0$$

Zero as a mathematical number

The ancient Egyptians and Greeks used zero as a placeholder, but its status as a number was cause for much debate. The first person to write down rules for using the number zero was the Indian mathematician Brahmagupta in 650 CE. Here are Brahmagupta's rules:

Today we think he was wrong about Rule 4. Mathematicians now say that you cannot divide a number by zero.

Scoring an egg

In sports, we need zero to keep the score, showing that one team or player hasn't scored yet.

In tennis, a player's score is called 'love' when they have yet to win a point in a game. This is from the French word 'l'eouf' meaning 'egg', because an egg is zero-shaped.

In cricket, a batsman who is out without scoring a run is said to have made a 'duck', after a duck's egg.

"Fifteen - love"

"Thirty - love"

"Quack quack"

Getting negative

As well as discovering rules for zero, Brahmagupta also found a meaning for negative numbers – numbers that are less than zero. He called negative numbers 'debts'. He called positive numbers 'fortunes'.

For the first time, there was a meaning to sums such as '5 – 7'. The answer, according to Brahmagupta, was 'debt 2', which we write down as '-2'.

Lining numbers up

We can write all the numbers, including positive numbers, zero and negative numbers, using a number line. Positive numbers are to the right and negative numbers to the left:

-10 -9 -8 -7 -6 -5 -4 -3 -2 -1

You can use a number line to work out long calculations. For instance, here we calculate 6 – 7 – 4 + 8
1. Start from zero and move 6 to the right

-10 -9 -8 -7 -6 -5 -4 -3 -2 -1

2. Move 7 to the left

-10 -9 -8 -7 -6 -5 -4 -3 -2 -1

3. Move 4 to the left

-10 -9 -8 -7 -6 -5 -4 -3 -2 -1

4. Finally move 8 to the right

-10 -9 -8 -7 -6 -5 -4 -3 -2 -1

How cold is it?

We need zero and negative numbers to tell the temperature. In the temperature scale Celsius, 0 is the freezing point of water, while 100 is the boiling point of water. Below 0 we need to use negative numbers.

On a thermometer, the height of the liquid shows the temperature. The lower the level, the colder it is. The scale is marked as a number line along the side. Two common scales are Fahrenheit (F) and Celsius (C).

The coldest air temperature ever found on the surface of Earth was -89.2°C, recorded in Antarctica on 21 July 1983. Most thermometers don't go down that low!

0 1 2 3 4 5 6 7 8 9 10

0 1 2 3 4 5 6 7 8 9 10

0 1 2 3 4 5 6 7 8 9 10

0 1 2 3 4 5 6 7 8 9 10

The answer is 3

0 1 2 **3** 4 5 6 7 8 9 10

Powers

Multiplying a number by itself is called taking the power of a number.

The square of 2 is

$$2 \times 2$$

It is written like this:

$$2^2 = 4 \ \square$$

(say 2 to the power of 2)

A number multiplied by its square is called a cube. For instance, the cube of 2 is

$$2 \times 2 \times 2$$

It is written like this

$$2^3 = 8$$

(say 2 to the power of 3)

We can repeat this process as many times as we want. The small numbers are called exponents, or powers.

For instance 2 to the power of 4,

$$2^4$$

means $2 \times 2 \times 2 \times 2 = 16$
Powers become very big very quickly. Here are some higher powers of 2:

$$2^6 = 64$$

$$2^{10} = 1,024$$

$$2^{20} = 1,048,576$$

Exponential power

To see how big powers can get, imagine you have a piece of paper that is 0.1 millimetre thick. Now cut the paper in half and place the pieces on top of one another. You have a pile 0.2 mm high. That's $2^1 \times 0.1$. Do this again to give you a pile 0.4 mm high ($2^2 \times 0.1$) and repeat the process another 98 times. You now have a stack of paper that is $2^{100} \times 0.1$ mm high.

0.1 mm thick

Written out in full, 2^{100} looks like this:

How many rounds?

You need exponents to work out how many players you can have in a knock-out tennis tournament. Working backwards, there will be 2^1 players in the final, 2^2 players in the semi-final, 2^3 players in the quarter-finals, and so on. In the main draw of Grand Slam tennis tournaments, there are seven rounds. This means that in the first round, there are 2^7 players, or 128.

1st Round

PLAYER 1 v PLAYER 2
PLAYER 3 v PLAYER 4
PLAYER 5 v PLAYER 6
PLAYER 7 v PLAYER 8
PLAYER 9 v PLAYER 10
PLAYER 11 v PLAYER 12
PLAYER 13 v PLAYER 14
PLAYER 15 v PLAYER 16
PLAYER 17 v PLAYER 18
PLAYER 19 v PLAYER 20
PLAYER 21 v PLAYER 22
PLAYER 23 v PLAYER 24
PLAYER 25 v PLAYER 26
PLAYER 27 v PLAYER 28
PLAYER 29 v PLAYER 30
PLAYER 31 v PLAYER 32
PLAYER 33 v PLAYER 34
PLAYER 35 v PLAYER 36
PLAYER 37 v PLAYER 38
PLAYER 39 v PLAYER 40
PLAYER 41 v PLAYER 42
PLAYER 43 v PLAYER 44
PLAYER 45 v PLAYER 46
PLAYER 47 v PLAYER 48
PLAYER 49 v PLAYER 50
PLAYER 51 v PLAYER 52
PLAYER 53 v PLAYER 54
PLAYER 55 v PLAYER 56
PLAYER 57 v PLAYER 58
PLAYER 59 v PLAYER 60
PLAYER 61 v PLAYER 62
PLAYER 63 v PLAYER 64
PLAYER 65 v PLAYER 66
PLAYER 67 v PLAYER 68
PLAYER 69 v PLAYER 70
PLAYER 71 v PLAYER 72
PLAYER 73 v PLAYER 74
PLAYER 75 v PLAYER 76
PLAYER 77 v PLAYER 78
PLAYER 79 v PLAYER 80
PLAYER 81 v PLAYER 82
PLAYER 83 v PLAYER 84
PLAYER 85 v PLAYER 86
PLAYER 87 v PLAYER 88
PLAYER 89 v PLAYER 90
PLAYER 91 v PLAYER 92
PLAYER 93 v PLAYER 94
PLAYER 95 v PLAYER 96
PLAYER 97 v PLAYER 98
PLAYER 99 v PLAYER 100
PLAYER 101 v PLAYER 102
PLAYER 103 v PLAYER 104
PLAYER 105 v PLAYER 106
PLAYER 107 v PLAYER 108
PLAYER 109 v PLAYER 110
PLAYER 111 v PLAYER 112
PLAYER 113 v PLAYER 114
PLAYER 115 v PLAYER 116
PLAYER 117 v PLAYER 118
PLAYER 119 v PLAYER 120
PLAYER 121 v PLAYER 122
PLAYER 123 v PLAYER 124
PLAYER 125 v PLAYER 126
PLAYER 127 v PLAYER 128

2nd Round
3rd Round
4th Round
Quarter final
Semi final
Final

1,267,650,600,228,229,401,496,703,205,376

After 100 doublings, your stack of paper would reach the most distant galaxy we can see through the Hubble Space Telescope, 13 billion light years away!

Making bases

The number system we use is called base 10 or decimal. There are 10 digits, 0–9, in each 'place' in the number system. The final digit represents the number of 'units', then each digit to the left is a power of 10 (10, 100, 1000...).

For example, the number

5,788 has

→ **5** Thousands

← **7** Hundreds

→ **8** Tens

← **8** Units

1,000	100	10	units
5	7	8	8

We have chosen base 10 because it's the highest we can count with both hands! But we can count in any base we like.

14

Count like a computer

Computers count in base 2, or binary numbers. With binary numbers, there are just two digits: 0 and 1. Inside a computer, this is represented by a kind of switch called a bit, which can be 'on' (**1**) or 'off' (**0**). A computer memory is made up of billions of bits.

In binary numbers, each place is a power of 2: For instance, here is the binary number

1001101

64	32	16	8	4	2	units
1	0	0	1	1	0	1

To convert binary number **1001101** to decimal, add all the numbers with a '1' above: **64 + 8 + 4 + 1**. So, 1001101 binary = 77 decimal.

Counting the time

The ancient Babylonians counted in base 60. We still use base 60 to count the passing of time during a day:

60 seconds
= 1 minute

60 minutes
= 1 hour

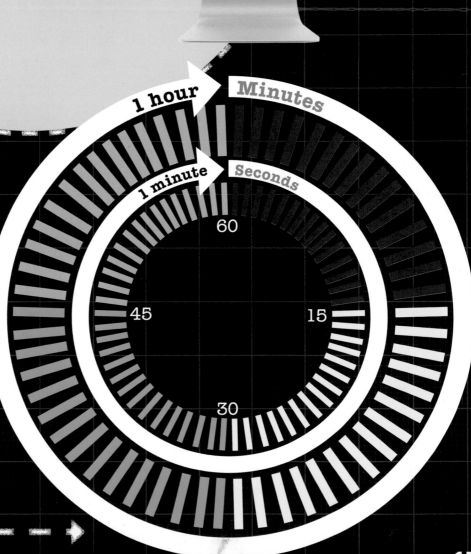

Big numbers

If you multiply 1,000 by 1,000, you get 1 million, which is a 1 with six 0s after it: 1,000,000, also written as 10^6. Multiply 1 million by 1000 and you get 1 billion, which is a 1 with nine 0s after it: 1,000,000,000, also written as 10^9.

Our Solar System

Distances in our Solar System are measured in thousands, millions or billions of kilometres.

The distance of Earth to the Sun, 150 million km, is called an Astronomical Unit, or AU. Astronomers use AU to describe big distances across the Solar System. The planet Neptune is about 30 AU from Earth.

Sun to Earth (1 AU)
150 million km

Moon to Earth
385,000 km (0.003 AU)

Neptune to Earth
4.3 billion km (30 AU)

People on Earth

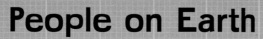

Tokyo, Japan, is the world's largest city. It has a population of **37 million**.

The biggest country in the world is **China**. It has over **1.4 billion** people. There are

7 billion people

on Earth, so 1 in every 5 people is Chinese.

The circumference of Earth at the equator is about 40,000,000 metres. If every person alive were lined up on the ground head-to-toe, they would circle Earth at the equator 300 times.

37 million

1.4 billion

Tokyo

China

Money, money, money

The richest people in the world are worth more than 1 billion US dollars and are called billionaires. In 2015, there were 1,800 billionaires. American computer tycoon Bill Gates was the richest of all. He was worth $79.2 billion. The very rich continue to get richer. The wealthiest 100 people in the world are as rich as the poorest 3 billion.

Really big numbers

Trillion (10^{12})
The distance light travels in a year, called a light year, is 9.4 trillion kilometres. The nearest star to our Sun, Alpha Centauri, is 4.4 light years away. That's about 41 trillion kilometres.

1 trillion = 1,000 billion

Quadrillion (10^{15})
The world's fastest computer, the Tianhe-2, can perform 34 quadrillion calculations per second.

1 quadrillion = 1,000 trillion

Quintillion (10^{18})
A Rubik's cube has 43 quintillion possible combinations.

1 quintillion = 1,000 quadrillion

Sextillion (10^{21})
In 1946, Hungary suffered a period of hyperinflation, meaning that its currency, the pengo, lost value dramatically. Hungarian banks started printing notes worth 1 sextillion pengo before they gave up on the pengo completely.

1 sextillion = 1,000 quintillion

Septillion (10^{24})
Earth has a mass of about 6 septillion kilogrammes.

1 septillion = 1,000 sextillion

Here's a neat trick for multiplying huge numbers.

If you want to work out $10^9 \times 10^{12}$, all you need to do is add together the exponents:

$$10^9 \times 10^{12}$$
$$= 10^{9+12}$$
$$= 10^{21}$$

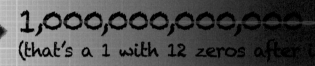
1,000,000,000,000
(that's a 1 with 12 zeros after it)

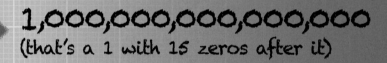
1,000,000,000,000,000
(that's a 1 with 15 zeros after it)

1,000,000,000,000,000,000
(that's a 1 with 18 zeros after it)

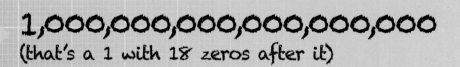
1,000,000,000,000,000,000,000
(that's a 1 with 21 zeros after it)

1,000,000,000,000,000,000,000,000
(that's a 1 with 24 zeros after it)

Really, really big numbers

The number 10^{100} – that's a 1 with 100 zeros after it – is called a googol. The name was made up by the nine-year-old nephew of American mathematician Edward Kasner (left). One googol is greater than the number of atoms in the whole universe.

Kasner imagined an even larger number – this is a 1 with a googol zeros after it. He called it a googolplex, and it is written in shorthand as $10^{10^{100}}$. There is not enough room in the whole universe to write out a googolplex in full.

1,000,
000,00
000,00
000,00

100

10

10

10

Search engine

The internet search engine Google is named after a spelling mistake. The company liked the idea of naming themselves after a really big number, but when they registered their website, someone typed in 'google' rather than 'googol', and the spelling stuck.

"How do you spell that then?"

"Erm, good question"

Then there is the googolplexplex. That's a 1 with a googolplex zeros after it,

or $10^{10^{10^{100}}}$! We would need more than a googol universes to write a googolplexplex out in full!

Rearranging the dust

Some numbers are so large that scientists must use their imaginations to find a way to describe them. Astronomer Carl Sagan imagined an entire universe filled with dust particles 1.5 millionths of a metre across. He worked out that the total number of ways that the dust could be arranged would equal about one googolplex.

To infinity

Whatever number you can think of, you can always make a bigger number by adding 1 or a smaller number by subtracting 1. This means that the number line goes on forever in both directions. We say that there is an infinite quantity of numbers.

Infinity is strange!

As infinity cannot be measured, it is not really a number. It is written using this symbol: ∞

Infinity has some strange properties. We can do certain calculations with it. For instance:

$$\infty + \infty = \infty$$

$$\infty \times \infty = \infty$$

$$\infty^{\infty} = \infty$$

But we cannot do other calculations. For instance,

$$\infty - \infty$$

cannot be worked out!

Is the Universe infinite?

Scientists do not know whether our Universe is infinitely big. Some think the Universe may be finite, but folded over on itself. This means that, if you travelled off in one direction, you would eventually find yourself back where you started, as if you were moving around the surface of a sphere.

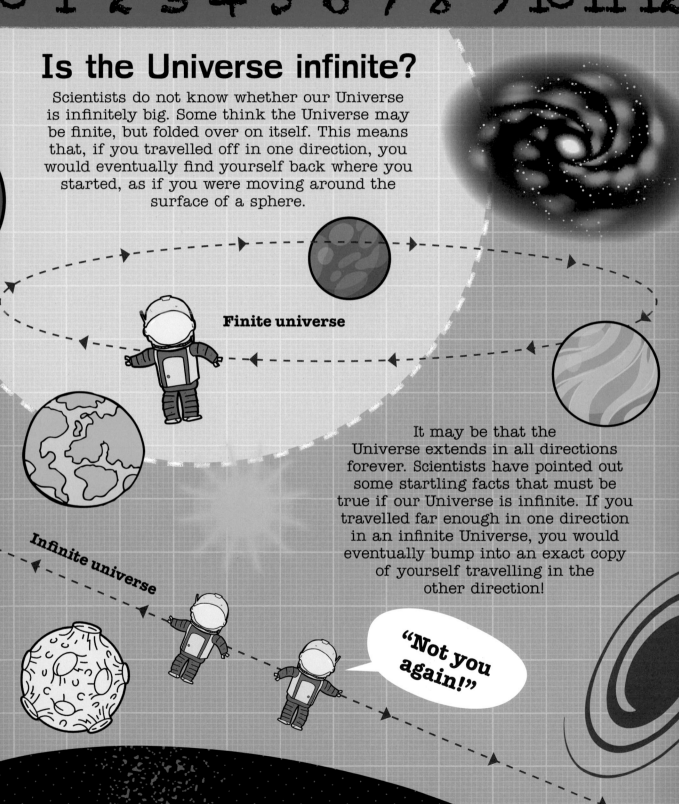

Finite universe

It may be that the Universe extends in all directions forever. Scientists have pointed out some startling facts that must be true if our Universe is infinite. If you travelled far enough in one direction in an infinite Universe, you would eventually bump into an exact copy of yourself travelling in the other direction!

Infinite universe

"Not you again!"

23

Strange numbers

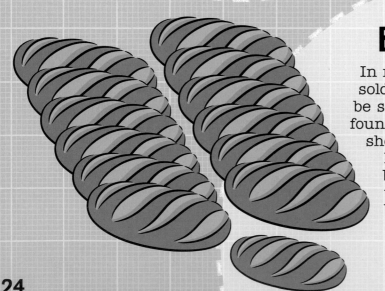

Count your bones

It is easy to count up to 12 using just one hand. Starting with your index finger, use your thumb to count off the bones in each of your fingers.

You have four fingers, each with three bones.

4 x 3 = 12

Dozens

A dozen is a group of 12 things. We often use the word 'dozens' to mean 'between about 20 and 90 things'. Counting in base 12 is called duodecimal.

Base 12 is easy to work with as 12 divides exactly by 6, 4, 3 and 2. We still buy some items, such as eggs, in groups of 4, 6 or 12.

Baker's dozen

In medieval England, bread was sold by weight, and bakers could be severely punished if they were found to be selling their customers short. Just in case any of their loaves were a little too light, bakers added an extra loaf to their orders. So if you asked a baker in 13th-century England for a dozen loaves, he would give you 13.

Roman numerals

If you think maths is hard today, spare a thought for the ancient Romans. They had a numeral system using letters that made some calculations very difficult indeed. We still use Roman numerals on clock faces, and you might also see them on the credits of old films and TV shows to say the year they were made.

1	2	3	4	5	6	7	8	9	10	50	100	500	1,000
I	II	III	IV	V	VI	VII	VIII	IX	X	L	C	D	M

A letter before another letter of greater value indicates 'minus':

IV = 5 − 1 = 4

A letter after another letter of greater value indicates 'plus':

VI = 5 + 1 = 6

So, for instance, what is the value of the Roman numeral

MDCCXCVI?

Working from the largest number to the left, we have:

M = 1,000
D = 500
CC = 2 x 100
= 200
XC = 100 − 10
= 90
VI = 5 + 1
= 6

Adding all these together, we get the value

1,796

Sums with Roman numerals

How do we do addition with such a strange system? For instance, what is the value of:

CCLXIV + DXXI = ?

This is not quite as difficult as it first appears. We first need to rewrite the sum without the 'minus' numerals. So we would rewrite IV as IIII. This gives:

CCLXIIII + DXXI

Next we line up all the symbols that appear in the sum, with the largest to the left:

DCCLXXXIIIII

Now combine all the symbols together that you can. For instance, **IIIII = V**. This gives our answer:

DCCLXXXV

Notice that we can do all this without ever working out what the numerals represent in our decimal number system! Converting to decimal, the sum looks like this:

264 + 521 = 785

Your body in numbers

You need many of the numbers in this book to describe what is going on in your body, although perhaps not the googolplex!

Amazing brains

The brain is just about the most complex object we know of.

→ A brain contains about **100 billion neurons.**

← Each neuron is connected to up to **10,000 other neurons.**

→ This means that your brain may have up to **1 quadrillion connections.**

Your brain makes connections every time you learn something new, so you should be making lots of new connections right now!

Beating hearts

An adult's heart beats about 70 times every minute. Kids' hearts beat a little faster. That means that your heart beats around 100,000 times in one day, and 35 million times in one year. If you live to the age of 85, your heart will beat 3 billion times in your lifetime. Animals' hearts beat at very different rates. Generally, the bigger the animal, the slower its heart rate. Here are human hearts compared to some other animals:

	Beats per minute	Lifespan (years)	Beats per lifetime
Human	70	85	3 billion
Cat	150	15	1.2 billion
Hamster	450	3	0.7 billion
Hummingbird	1,200	4	2.5 billion
Bowhead whale	20	up to 250	2.6 billion

How long have you been alive?

On your **tenth birthday**, you have been alive for:

↓

10 years

↓

120 months

↓

3,652 days
(including two leap years!)

↓

87,648 hours

↓

5,258,880 minutes

↓

315,532,800 seconds

At some point near the end of the second week of the ninth month after your 31st birthday, you will have been alive for exactly **1 trillion seconds**.

A growing baby

Your body contains 100 trillion cells. They have all grown from one fertilised egg inside your mother's womb. The cells divide every 12 to 24 hours, leading to exponential growth in the number of cells.

At **conception**, there is **one cell**.

After **12 hours**, it divides into **two cells**.

After **3 days**, there are **12 cells**.

After **3 weeks**, the embryo contains more than **1 billion cells**.

After **3 months**, the foetus is taking human shape and is already made up of more than **1 trillion cells**.

Body bacteria

For every cell in your body, there are also at least 10 bacteria. So your body contains around

1 quadrillion bacteria.

Many of them are in your gut and help you digest your food.

Quiz

1 Which **number** is represented by the beads on each of these abacuses?

a)

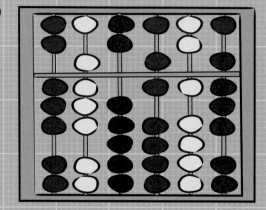

b)

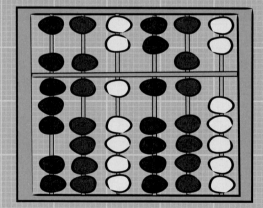

c)

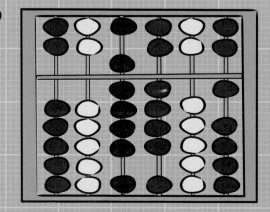

2 Write out the **number line** above, and use it to work out the following sums:

a) $4 + 5 - 9 + 2$

b) $9 - 14 + 8 + 5$

c) $^{-}7 + 5 + 3 + 9$

3 a) Four of the following eight numbers are **prime numbers**. Can you find them?

$3, 5, 7, 15, 21, 29, 49, 87$

b) Each of the four **non-prime numbers** can be made by multiplying two of the primes together. How?

4 Convert the following binary numbers into **decimal**:

a) 101

b) 11010

c) 110001

5 Convert the following decimal numbers into **binary**:

a) 7

b) 16

c) 25

28

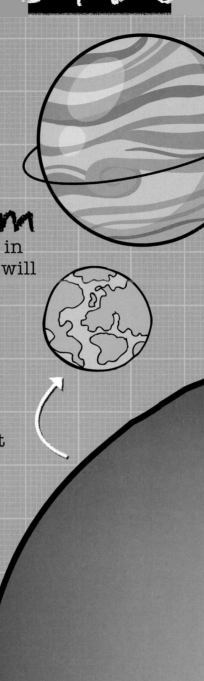

6 What are the **values** of the following powers:

a) 2^3

b) 10^2

c) 3^4

7 A piece of paper is **1 mm** thick. If you fold the paper in half four times, **how thick** will the folded paper be?

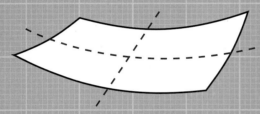

8 You are planning a knockout football tournament with five rounds. **How many** teams will take part in the first round?

9 At its closest point, Jupiter is about

750 million

kilometres from the Sun. Taking one Astronomical Unit (AU) as 150 million km, **how many times farther** from the Sun is Jupiter than Earth?

10 The space probe *Voyager 1* was launched in 1977. By 2015, it was 130 AU from Earth. **How many billions** of kilometres had it travelled?

11 What are the **names** of the following huge numbers?

a) 10^{12}

b) 10^{18}

c) $10^{10^{100}}$

12 You have been asked to go to the shop to buy

five-dozen eggs.

The eggs are sold in cartons with six eggs each. **How many cartons** do you need to buy?

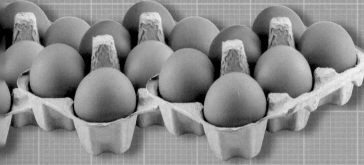

13 These years are written out in Roman numerals. What years are they?

a) DLI

b) MMI

c) MMIX

14 On a clock with Roman numerals, the hour hand is pointing at **VII** and the minute hand is pointing at **XII**. What time is it?

15 What is the answer to this sum in **Roman numerals**?

MIV + XIII

16 If there are 7 billion people on Earth and each person's body is made up of 100 trillion cells, **how many human cells** are there on Earth?

17 A rat's average heart rate is

400 beats

per minute. If it lives for exactly 3 years, **how many times** will its heart beat in its lifetime?
Hint: First work out how many beats in a day, then how many in a year.

Glossary

Bacteria
Tiny single-cell life forms that are just a few millionths of a metre across. Bacteria are the most common form of life on Earth.

Base
The number of different digits used in a counting system. Decimal numbers are base 10, which means that they use ten different digits.

Binary
A counting system that uses base 2. Computers count in binary.

Boiling point
The temperature at which a substance turns from a liquid into a gas. The boiling point of water is 100°C.

Cell
The smallest basic unit that makes up living things. Nearly all living things start life as a single cell.

Decimal
A counting system that uses base 10.

Digit
A symbol used to write down numbers. In the decimal system, there are ten digits: 0–9.

Equator
An imaginary line around Earth. The equator forms a circle that is the same distance from the North and South poles. It is 40,075 km long.

Exponential growth
Growth in which the rate of increase is proportional to the size of the value. Repeated doubling in size is an example of exponential growth.

Freezing point
The temperature at which a substance turns from a liquid into a solid. The freezing point of water is 0°C.

Hyperinflation
A period in which a currency loses value very quickly as prices rise. A doubling in the price of goods every few days will produce hyperinflation through exponential growth.

Lunar month
The length of time between two full moons or two new moons, as seen from Earth. A lunar month varies between 29.2 days and 29.9 days, with an average length of 29.5 days.

Neuron
Also called a nerve cell, a neuron is a special kind of cell that transmits electrical signals to other cells. The brain is made up of billions of neurons, which form a complex network of ever-changing connections.

Power
Also called an exponent, a number that tells you how many times to use another number in a multiplication. For example in 2^4, the power is 4, meaning 'multiply 2 four times'.

Index

Answers

1. a) 380,618 b) 861,160 c) 9,401
2. a) 2 b) 8 c) 10
3. a) 3, 5, 7 and 29 are prime
  b) $15 = 5 \times 3$; $21 = 7 \times 3$; $49 = 7 \times 7$; $87 = 29 \times 3$
4. a) 5 b) 26 c) 49
5. a) 111 b) 10000 c) 11001
6. a) 8 b) 100 c) 81
7. The paper will be 2^4 mm thick, which is 16 mm.
8. 2^5 players, which is 32.
9. Jupiter is 5 AU from the Sun. Earth is 1 AU from the Sun. So Jupiter is 5 times farther from the Sun than Earth.
10. 4.5 billion kilometres = 150 million × 130
11. a) Trillion b) Quintillion c) Googolplex
12. 10 cartons
13. a) 551 b) 2001 c) 2009
14. It is 7 o'clock
15. MXVII
16. 7 billion × 100 trillion = $(7 \times 10^9) \times (100 \times 10^{12}) = 700 \times 10^{9+21} = 700 \times 10^{21}$. So there are 700 sextillion human cells on Earth.
17. 0.63 billion times